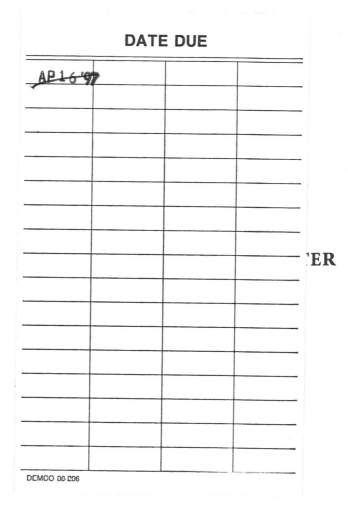

DATE DUE

AP 16 '97		

'ER

DEMCO 08-206

THE SUNSHINE MINE DISASTER

JAMES BROCK

UNIVERSITY OF IDAHO PRESS
MOSCOW, IDAHO
1995

98 97 96   5 4 3 2

LIBRARY OF CONGRESS CATALOGING-IN-PUBLICATION DATA
BROCK, JAMES, 1958-
    THE SUNSHINE MINE DISASTER/JAMES BROCK.
        P.   CM.
    ISBN 0-89301-181-9
        1. SUNSHINE MINE DISASTER, KELLOGG, IDAHO, 1972 — POETRY. 2.
SILVER MINES AND MINING — IDAHO — KELLOGG — POETRY.
3. MINE ACCIDENTS — IDAHO — KELLOGG — POETRY. 4. SILVER MINERS —
IDAHO — KELLOGG — POETRY.   I. TITLE.
PS3552.R59S86   1995
811'.54—DC20   95-36471
                                                    CIP

Cover Photo: Beth Rumpel
Sunshine Mine Memorial erected May 1974, Big Creek near
Kellogg, Idaho.

For Dene and Alice,
for Carson,
my first book,
with gratitude and love,
and in memorium,
for the ninety-one miners.

CONTENTS

PREFACE

It is somewhat irregular for a poet to include a preface to a collection of poems; after all, the poetry should be able to speak for itself. But what I've written here is neither simply a collection of poems nor a history of a significant event in Idaho's past. Yes, there's poetry and history here, but my objective in writing this book wasn't to write poetry or history. Quite simply, something had disturbed me, something very much like the dead who occasionally bother to speak to us, something I had to answer to.

Much of the book is poetry. Much of the book is found artifact: the Lola letters, the "Brautigan-inspired" lyrics, the interview between James McParland and Harry Orchard, the Bill Haywood case, the Danny Taylor report. And much of the book is fact, in as much as reporters record fact from primary sources. Thus I culled information from articles in *The Atlantic Monthly, The New York Times, The Idaho Statesman, The Lewiston Tribune,* from a variety of histories and narratives on silver mining in Idaho, and from biographies and autobiographies of Clarence Darrow, Big Bill Haywood, Harry Orchard, and William E. Borah. I also relied upon my personal memories and knowledge, having been a thirteen-year-old in Boise when the disaster occurred. Perhaps this book is more of an example of life-writing than it is poetry.

And while I did not alter the facts as I discovered them, I obviously shaped them to the truth of fiction. For instance, the main character, Dan Taylor, is a fiction. As far as I know, no man survived in the shafts for eight days, only to die one day before being rescued. The only immediate survivors are, of course, Tom Wilkinson and Ron Flory, the two who lived seven days in the mine after the fire, drinking water from the condensation of the air conditioners and eating the lunches remaining in their buddies' lunch pails, and who were rescued alive. And yet, I choose the perspective of Dan Taylor to dominate the book, his voice beginning and ending the sequence, almost always the "I" of the opening and closing sections, and it is his life I focus on: his grandmother, his parents, his brother, his wife, his son. Other perspectives enter in, and I do refer to real miners, their spouses, and their children. I have kept the actual names of some; other names

I conflated. I tried to keep the names intact, but the more I tried, the more they coalesced. And so I yielded, perhaps wishing to be true to the way the dead lose their individuality, the way I cannot separate and distinguish ninety-one deaths, the way the dead become the vanished, thousands of feet underground with too much monoxide and smoke to recover and reclaim them. I pray that I have not offended the living relatives by these changes.

Finally, I wish to express gratitude to those who encouraged me with this collection over the years. Thank you, Annette Sisson, Don Boes, Jane Hilberry, Pam Wampler, Kimberly Carlson, and Gerri Reaves. Thank you to Joe Calandriello for the Lola letters. I also wish to recognize the National Endowment for the Arts, the Tennessee Arts Commission, and the Alex Haley Foundation for fellowships that gave me the time and the confidence to try to do something important. To you, the readers for the University of Idaho Press, William Studebaker, Ron McFarland, and Roger Mitchell (you, old friend), I am indebted for your advice. I am most grateful for your nerve, Peggy Pace. And to Maggie Ward, wherever you are, thank you for teaching me that in Idaho, too, there is poetry.

James Brock
Pocatello, Idaho
15 October 1994

CHORALE FOR PRAISE

—after Melville

Today we asked the captain
         what course he proposed
to take toward a beast
         so large, terrifying, terrible.
He hesitated, then answered:
         "I think I shall praise it."

I. THE SMOKE

"Do you know what it is like now? It's like a living graveyard."

—Alice Hillman (widow of
Howard Hillman, aged 34, who
died of carbon monoxide
poisoning in the disaster)

4

If a man doesn't
like to rush, and I don't,
he can spend a half
hour in the dry-house:
pull on his T-shirt,
overalls, wool socks,
steel-toed rubber boots,
helmet, belt, battery pack
and light, a denim
jacket. And still time
to make good daylight
at 6:30 a.m. in Big Creek
Canyon. Most Mays, upon
the ridge above the Crescent
Mine, you can see ten
or twelve head of elk
below the snow line. It's
easy, in this work,
to think of cave paintings
when you see wildlife
in the dawn's light, before
pounding the face with
dynamite, mucking out
the rock, clearing the new
ground. But I don't like
that kind of confusion.

Extraction counts for nothing
save the pay dirt; and those
paintings are just some lines,
guttural and round, copies
of animals that had
come out of nowhere
and had nowhere to go
on this slow earth. Today
three elk appear, two females and
a calf, feeding off the greening
bitter-brush. To the calf
I say, "Grow fat,
you bastard," as I measure
the distances of two
Octobers with a thumb,
a hair cross-sight.

What do you expect?
        Once you've chiseled out
110 miles of tunnel and backdrift,
    you got to have a place
            for refuse: rotten timber, ratty

clothes, broken tools. It's
            natural to bury what you
don't need, what you can
    no longer use. So take a dead-
            end shaft or a worked-out

drift, a direction that was bad
            from the word go, and you fill
it, and cork it with a bulkhead.
    Clean. Anything
            under pressure burns, but always

a cold fire on account of low
            air, always the slow stuff
of decay heatening up. You
    can't expect spontaneous
            combustion. And

once it goes, it is never the fire,
              but the boiling monoxide
that will kill you quick as sin,
      and all you got is a twelve-man
            hoister, one half-hour, and

five thousand feet. Take
            Big Pete Eilerts, among the first
to die, after so much life whoring
      and unemployed, with a wife
            resigned to sleep with other miners

to get pregnant: would you expect
            such a strong man to pray, so
near the bulkhead, so close a goner,
      over a fire so small?
            God help you.

THE SELF-RESCUERS (THE MONOXIDE CONVERTERS)

The blueing poisoning air backdrafts down the drift, leaving
halos and fingers
of smoke over the bodies of two of the dead: Wiederrich
and McCoy. The self-rescuers
spat from their mouths, rusted out, too slow in converting CO
to CO_2, lay
upon the dirt, coiling out an expanse
of breath.

Alice Hillman's potato salad
is third in line. First milk.
Sandwiches. Then what follows
is tupperwared: tuna, macaroni,
angel food cake. The fruit,
oranges and apples, can
be saved. It is spring.
Coffee.

      The bodies have become
clay upon the grounding rock.
Howard Hillman's face is clay.
I could not take his lunch pail
until the last heat slipped out of him,
which took time, as what he said
was true, that he looks big
enough to eat oats and pull
a plow, even with one lung
gone and the other dusted
with emphysema. The mounds
of waxed paper make faces. I take
these remains: a Baby Ruth bar
and the potato salad.

I do not believe in saying
grace. The potato salad is sponge.
I will not remember July

or Day's Cafe or Yellow Pine
when I eat it. The mine takes
things from you. Someday, too soon,
I will have to thank Alice.

I pull the coat
off my brother's body.
I want to believe
it died of shock, not what
the face confirms, a seizure
of monoxide. The lining
is the color of silver. In sun,
the silver would run
maroon between my fingers.
For once, this would
be enough, to be draped
within the coat Dad
gave Mark, after beating
him, for running, for
following my tracks
to the mines, for giving
up school. He is dead
and blackening in the dark.
I pull the coat on.
I am not afraid.

It didn't take Georgia O'Keeffe
to tell him a flower
was sex. Among the regenerative fires
of zinnias and snapdragons,
how could a man not see
the beauty of the pistil,
the bee, the mouth, the vagina,
all combusting in a radial of air
and blue? Now, as my father
tills his garden, thousands
of feet above, furrowing the earth,
cutting closer to me by inches,
and all I really know of him
is dream, I dream him
as the grapevine that works
its way through lattices,
and so full of leaf, fruit,
that I wake, knowing
gardens are sorrow and love,
like fathers. I wake,
unsure if it is in a son
to forgive the parent
who has learned to graft
the residue of cuttings. I wake
to listen for my brother's breathing,

the sound of old life growing
close. I hear only my own
rasping. I know no finer art
than dreaming. Before this dream
leaves, I will name it
"My Father, beside His Garden,"
or "Idaho, Last Summer." Before
this dream leaves, I whisper, Father,
how fast my dreams flee,
how slow your gardens grow.

Cradled in the statue of my mother,
I cradle my son in the quieting night,
singing mother's lullaby, Dickinson's
poetry, a trick of timing I have learned
to glide across the caesura:
It's in the breathing.
                    In my breathing,
I have learned to regulate my son's weight
in my arms, his ten months
pressing, a grasping, an unwillingness
to release the toy I stupidly offered
for love, for the quiet. With a lowing
breath, I offer homilies, how desire
means death, how poems are about fire,
meaning for him to touch the door first
before setting foot.
                    "The accent
of a coming Foot—/ The opening of a Door—"
I sing Dickinson, and though I hold my son,
I listen for fire, for a ghost, knowing
the house is empty. He falls asleep
before I sing my favorite lines—"The revery
alone will do, / If bees are few"—and
I embrace his sleeping body, still cradled
in my mother's arms, swaying to the metronome
of her rocking, her breathing, between the love
and the quiet, cradled in her statue.

Early in July
the maple leaves grew larger
    than my face, and I watched
them from the tree house where
    at night I slept, I
blanketed by leaf-shadow in moonlight.
    There was only surrender.

I would wake
to the hushed thuds of hardwood
    doors. Below me Mr. Moorehouse,
the landlord, forbade my mother
    to enter his house. Above them
as if nature had lost all concern, Mrs. Moorehouse
    lay—I saw the amber

of her room
dusted—dying in the hours before
    morning. I was not allowed
to go to funerals; if
    I were, I would have seen
Mr. Moorehouse stern with muscle
    and nerve, hating

a woman he lived with
for thirty years, his son
   from Los Angeles crying,
crying. Worn pine planks he nailed
   over her window. Why cover
so cruelly the warmest vestige of memory?
   I still cannot say.

   Or I would
climb down, Mother calling my name
   in two syllables,
"Da-an!" In her kitchen, she sliced
   potatoes thin, her face
white and secret, another death stored
   from me. Her stillborn,

   five years younger
than I. After a birthday I could never
   own that year, a nurse
from the hospital came, her hair cut
   like Natalie Wood's.
She picked me up, telling me
   how good

   I was, what
nice dimples I had. That
   was in December.
Then in June and for requiem
   (as I now think)
we moved to Lewiston's Orchards,
   a greener

less shadowed place.
There my parents' trees drew
   from dams: peach
and box elder. Every August, I
   climbed my three-rung
ladder, the branches too brittle to hold
   me, and the peaches

   so full they
bruised under their own weight; I
   tore them with a slight
twist. Mother quartered them. Father
   scooped french vanilla ice
cream. In a wet year, the peach tree
   died of root fungus.

   And this morning,
a second floor apartment housed
   me; beyond my kitchen
window, a grackle ate a crab apple.
   The bird tore the May-born
skin. The black head rocked back.
   Crab apple slid down

   its throat. Again
living in trees, how I remember
   their growing out of dying,
wrapped in dead bark, and how

our mutual living—the grackle's
and mine—must, must, must
  be so wrapped

  by death.
The grackle dropped its head, stopped,
  and leaned into flight.
I watched the black bird fly
  in a fear I too
sensed. Where the fruit hung,
  the limb still quivered.

  If I owned
a brass pocket telescope, tonight I would
  climb a childhood tree:
maple, and I'd look through my neighbor's
  window to see if they're
not dead yet, to see them as alive and
  new as leaves.

CONSTELLATIONS:

TWO APPARITIONS OF LOLA ROBERTS

The compressed air line
hisses out the tap, and I
would shut it if I could,
if not for the sleeplessness,
the suffocation, and the visions.
Of late, I have seen the ghost
of my grandmother, Lola Roberts Taylor,
a Catholic who corrected me
in saying, "it's *the* Coeur
d'Alenes, not Coeur d'Alene,"
and who took credit
for civilizing May Arkwright Hutton
and the better part
of Spokane (the Jesuits
came later, she claimed). I
do not know any of this, but
that she has made manifestations.
Once at twilight, behind the Wallace
Avenue Sinclair station,
in the oil that bled down
a granite slag, Lola's face appeared.
Iridescent tears formed beneath

her eyes, silvering the rock. She

whispered, "Hell is life without

God. Go ahead. Try to live
as if there were no God, and
you'll see what I mean."
That time there were no witnesses.
The vision laughed a little,
disappeared.

      In a better darkness,
the stars that form the spine
Ursa Minor are visible
to the naked eye. I can remember
whom I last told of Ursa
Minor's dormant stars: Eleanor
Boyce. And it was a time
of a better darkness. Despite
the Idaho sky with the Milky
Way as its one low lying cloud,
neither one of us could connect
the stars that outlined the little bear.
Neither in that wilderness—with
or without God—did we feel
humanly frail. Despair did not
drive us to make love. We left
the mountains, winding home, our faces
touched and held green upon the
windshield.

      Now, it is Lola
Roberts, eighteen and almost virginal,
who reveals herself in my palms.

It is not any face I remember frayed
in the silver grain of photographs, but
of someone else stiffened by loss,
a sailor turned Wobbly left for dead
in Chelan. I press my lips to the cup
of my hand and drink. I do not taste
the pure sorrow for the regenerate
and the sinful. I taste nothing. It is
only a vision, a little bear too faint to see.

FROM FOUR LETTERS TO MISS LOLA
ROBERTS OF WARDEN, IDAHO

U.S.S. CHATTANOOGA

BREST, FRANCE

AUG. 31, 1919

Dearest Lola—:

It is quite a pleasure to be home once more and
have the opportunity of writing to you. I found your
letter waiting for me. I don't know where to begin.

My stay in Paris was really a battle, too. In one
sense, Paris is a gay city, but even a faster city than
our New York. So there are some bad morals here.
And wild women. I have never seen so many in all
my life. And so temptation I had it on all sides. I do
not know whether I survived it or not. We sail from
here to England and then to someplace in Norway,
so I hear.

Lola, I do not know how to do this best, so I'll
be plain spoken. I think far more of you than as a
friend and would like to know if I hold a position
above the average in your life. I may be foolish in
writing this way, but I cannot help it. I often think
how nice it would be to have something to look for-
ward to. If I be wrong, forgive me.

Till next time,

Jesse French

U.S.S. Chattanooga

at sea

Nov. 20, 1919

Dear Lola—:

I wish it could have been so that I could have been at Warden to attend the revival meeting you wrote about. The last church I was in with services going on was Notre Dame in Paris. It did me no good. In a few months, I'll be in civilian dress, starting out life in what capacity I do not know. Something might happen to pass. I don't know if I can go back to the mines.

In England, I have been trying to learn how to dance, but I am a poor scholar and wish I had started younger. American music is all the go here.

Au revoir,

Jesse

24

U.S.S CHATTANOOGA

PORT EDGAR, SCOTLAND

MARCH 17, 1920

Dear Lola—:

We are here in bonnie Scotland to take over
some German ships—the S. M. S. Frankfort and
some destroyers tomorrow night. I am to be skipper
of the Frankfort with a crew of four. Not bad for a
land-locked boy. How would you like to visit my
ship? She is a nice light cruiser and as clean as one
can expect her after spending many days on the bot-
tom of Scapa Floe.

You say you do not dance and would not care
to learn. As far as I can see there is no more harm in
dancing than in playing basketball. But of course, I
can only speak the man's part and think from expe-
rience that when I dance with a girl my thoughts of
her are just as clean as if I were in conversation with
her. But I will admit there are people whose minds
are degenerated and of low order and drink. Makes
things worse. I am glad America is dry.

Yours as ever,

Jesse

MULLAN, IDAHO

AUG. 11, 1920

Dear Lola—:

Just a few lines.
If nothing happens I would like to come
down Sunday as I am back in this part of the world
and I am not sure of what next. I have to get
started doing something or go dizzy or something
worse. I am surprising you, as I am not going to
stop writing you, unless I ship over in the navy or
join the federation and I hope it is a cold day in
August when I do. As I can talk sometimes more
than I can write, I will close.

As ever yours,

Jesse

Only the tombstones—all stained limestone—
were what the jimson weed and winter grass
could not reclaim. Tracing the rough calligraphy

of a name, I conjured a face, any face
of my own distant beloveds: my parents,
or my brother, but it came to nothing, or at best

I recalled my first home in photographs,
sawtooth-edged and framed by dates scrawled
in my mother's hand. A place in an old

suburb—even with a twenty-five year
mortgage paid, even with walls pockmarked
by love and failure—is as hollow

as when it was built. I recalled when at three
I sometimes left my brother's room
and slept between my father's and mother's

bodies. I could remember everyone.
I came upon the cemetery's last burial:
Lola Margaret Roberts Taylor, who died June 7,

1948 at the age of 53. My living, unregenerate
heart almost laughed, but over these forsaken
I wanted to believe Lola, of whom I never

knew, of whom was blood, who had mastered
her own love, discovering with her warm flesh
the pleasures of her warm flesh. With that,

I grieved over her absence: someday, the child
my wife and I have begot, a man
we do not know, will have to order

the tombstones inscribed with our names,
our dates of births and deaths, and bury us
somewhere near our resting parents, our bodies

somewhere between theirs cradled in the binding
earth. I touched Lola's name, the hollow
marks of her perfect life. I felt no chill.

Only the slightest, the first October breeze
with bones in it touched my face.

SUN IN AN EMPTY ROOM:

DAN AND ELEANOR, 1968

In his parents' home, two sixteen-year-olds
have made love for the first time. The boy rises, and
he pinches the base of the condom, stopping
the backflow of semen. She turns from the bed,
reaching for her purse, and she grabs some Kleenex
to clean the blood from her pubic hair, her inner thighs.
The girl stares at the boy. Three feet of sunlight
separate them: the boy drops the condom
in a waste bucket, and each alone reclaims
his and her body, dressing without speech, and they
leave the room, holding one another. That night
in bed together, one dreams of sun in an empty room,
the sun bequeathing shape and warmth on the walls.
The other dreams of red horses. Upon waking,
they walk through the nearly legible light of morning;
beginning to love, they hear the wane
of their threading voices, filling an empty room,
those first sounds of the incompleted living.

I dream of the last steelhead run.
I dream of the operatic bolts
    of silver halving the water, slivers
    of instinct, the smell of birth.
I dream of the dog-faced black bears,
    of how skinny they are
    in Idaho, the drunken reel
    of their bodies, pawing
    at the foam, the sun-silken
    flashes.
I dream of the way you, my lover,
    and I work the poles, the way
    you tear the fleshy eggs
    and wrap them around the hooks.
I dream the steelhead run.
I dream bears.
I dream the want of scent.
Tonight.
Your hands.

30

When I escape the mine,
Walter Cronkite asks,
"Who is your hero? What
inspired you to survive?"
I say, "I have two heroes:
Richard Brautigan and
Evel Knievel. When I
graduated from Lewiston
High School, my English
teacher gave me a copy
of *The Pill Versus the Spring
Hill Mining Disaster*. I've
come to write two poems
inspired by Brautigan, who
I'm told lives above the mining
country of Butte, Montana.
Evel Knievel is also
from Montana. Did you
know that? I loved Evel
ever since he said,
'Don't try this at home.'
But I did and I do.
I swear he will jump
the Snake River someday.

When he does, I'll rev up
my Honda 750 cc and jump
the goddamn mouth of the
Lucky Friday mine. After that,
I can then return to Eleanor,
father more children, and
teach them how not to let go
of a bike in mid-air. Read
them some poems. Quit
smoking so much dope."

THE FIRST DAN TAYLOR POEM INSPIRED BY RICHARD BRAUTIGAN, 1971

Writing a Poem at 6:00 a.m. while my Lover Fondles my Penis

I have two choices.

THE SECOND DAN TAYLOR POEM INSPIRED BY RICHARD BRAUTIGAN, 1971

Horse Steak Meadow (a prairie in northern Idaho named by Lewis & Clark)

I wonder what happened
to the rest of Trigger
after he was stuffed.

Walter, this is what I must
    make of the sounding
of smoke. For days I live

dreaming of you. "How did
    you survive for seven days?"
you'll ask. I promise not

to remember the now, the taste
    of this processed cheese, the breaking
loose of fingers on lunch pails.

I have eaten too much ghost food.
    There's too much I owe,
Walter. That's why I think I

must live. And I'll wait for the Sunshine
    Mine Disaster Reunion. Five
years. Ten years. Twenty-five years.

It will be as big as death. As
    big as Walter Cronkite in Idaho.
Maybe bigger.

I remember how we would imitate
Evel: jackknifing stolen bikes
out into the St. Joe, our arms
lifted up, and we'd fall, wingless,
and two splashes into the deep.
Most bikes would last five jumps.

Above me, Byron Schulz is the last
to get out, trucking from the 3100-foot
level, having brought up loads
of sixteen dead and seven alive.
At a thousand feet, he meets
the rescue crew, and they share
their oxygen masks. Don Beechner,
the next-to-last to die, pulls off
his mask for Schulz. Don falls down,
the monoxide evaporating his lungs,
blood gushing from his nose, and
he is dead beneath Byron's breathing.

I remember two years ago, Eleanor
and I watching the draft lottery,
and my birthday came up, and
the lieutenant colonel on television
matched it to 258. We wouldn't
have to marry yet, I wouldn't have

to run to college. And we made love
there, he calling out, "June 9, 41 . . .
August 17, 7 . . . December 2, 113 . . ."

This, I dare not imagine:
Eleanor cleans out the drawers,
and there she finds my last
papers: two poems, a fourth-grade report,
a photograph of some kids, letters
addressed to my grandmother,
a registration card for the draft. And
she places them back, the air still
too full of octaves, under all that silence,
under the abstinence.

THE RAINBOW TROUT IN IDAHO,

AN ILLUSTRATED REPORT

BY DANNY TAYLOR   *37*

FOR MRS. ROETHIG

GRADE 4

APRIL 7, 1962

Idaho and the Rainbow Trout

Fish abound in Idaho's streams and lakes. The Snake River and its tributaries have fishable runs of oceangoing steelhead, salmon, and sturgeon. Pend O'Reille Lake is noted as the home of the kokanee, a landlocked salmon, and of the deepwater kamloops trout, a relative of the rainbow trout. Bass and trout are taken throughout the state, as are other game species such as perch, crappie, and bluegill. The largest hatchery of rainbow trout eggs in the United States is located near Hagerman, on the Snake River, in Elmore County.

The Feeding of Adults in a Fish Hatchery

The water is essentially used as a support for the fish, and all the food is supplied from the outside. Japanese shrimp culture and trout raising in the United States are prominent examples of this type of feeding.

THE RAINBOW TROUT

The Rainbow Trout, *Salmo Gairdnerii*, was native to almost the total length of the North American Pacific Coast. The Rainbow Trout varies in color, often blending in with its surroundings. Rainbow Trout often migrate to the sea when they are about two years old. They are then known as Steelhead Trout. In salt water, it gradually becomes a uniform steely blue or silvery, and the pink band is very light or invisible.

CONCLUSION

Everything comes from *The Encylopedias Americana*. But the books dont say nothing about the Redfish which is a Rainbow. That's what my Dad says. Also if you hold a Rainbow too long and get the silver on your hands. The trout will die when you put it back in the river. That goes for the Redfish and the Regular Rainbow Trout too.

The Rainbow Trout

If a planter, this fin is cut off.

BEFORE THE RESCUE: A LITTLE MELODRAMA, A LITTLE DREAM

After the villain has tied the girl
to the train tracks and she's free
     enough to scream, corseted in rope

    from her knees to her breasts,
and still helpless, and it's before
     any rescue, before the steam engine

    breaches the bend, with so much
time alone that she begins to see
     nothing but herons flood the sky,

    blueing and orangeing and greening
the air above her. They are gentle
     gliders, all male, quieting, and they

    look at her, each one, with eyes
that brim with responsibility. She has
     never seen birds so content. Soon

the sky reclaims itself, leaving one
female heron to circle over her, and

the heron drops one egg, mid air,
      one hundred feet up, shouting, "Catch!

Catch! Catch!" Opening her free
hand inches above the rail, she feels
      the break of the egg's falling, and

she clasps the egg, a smooth jewel.
Before the heat of the train's coming
      vibrates against her neck, after

the villain has given up hope of his
marrying her and has hit the road
      rifling through other mortgages

of virgins to foreclose, the girl allows
herself one vow: when the train wrecks
      its wheels against her body, she shall

hold onto this gift, willing the egg
never to crack, nesting it forever
      in the skeleton of her palm.

Upon my graduation, my mother gave
me an album, and everything I
recognized, except for the photograph,
"At Spirit Lake, Washington, 1961,"
five kids, a woman, somewhere between
Kelso and Mount St. Helens, on a stump.
I don't know any of them, only guessing
they are versions of cousins or neighbors
in a light that now abrades their faces.

And somewhere, too, I know my face
is locked as a stranger in a relative's
or school mate's photograph, someone forgotten
or never known, a piece of human
clutter: the boy in the station
wagon, the teenager at the dance,
the man tossing the cigarette butt. I
know I fill in too many places for my own
good, occupy too many geographic
centers of ghost towns, my image firmed,
youthful and grainy. In pictures, I am
always youthful and strange in a silvering
light whose beauty anyone would covet.
Someone who once knew me might point
to my image and ask, "Isn't that Mark?," and
while dead wrong, wouldn't be too far off.

43

The smoke, I have begun to think, rolls
in blankets. That is a metaphor, I know,
a slip knot of language. Still, the smoke
rolls over, above the stope, and the pearled

visitations that accompany the dying
invade my waking. I see Eleanor, one year
ago, her seven months of pregnancy
pulling me in, sleeping, her body a liquid

K, propped by pillows. I place my hand
on her belly and wait for morning to come.
Already I know how these metaphors
thin, but how else can I face my lost faith

in buried lives, except to erect scaffolding,
a heart large enough to house its want?

II. IDAHO SILVER

"God brought us back for a purpose. Me and Ron
are gonna do a lot of people a lot of good. Things are gonna be
changed, not just here but all over the country."

—Tom Wilkinson (with

Ron Flory, the two miners who

survived the accident, after being

trapped for six days)

"Kellogg's all right if you don't want to make
anything of your life. After this, maybe people will get a new
perspective. But after a while, it will go back to the way it was."

—Kathi Farley (17 at the

time of the accident, who would

leave Kellogg to go to college and

write poetry)

A LITTLE HISTORY: HARRY ORCHARD KILLS FORMER GOVERNOR FRANK STEUNENBERG, DECEMBER 30, 1905

The bomb itself means little: a combination
of dynamite, plaster of paris, chloride
of potash, some sugar, and a fishing line
to set the detonator. The papers
get it wrong, nothing to do with "an explosive
placed with such devilish ingenuity
that a Russian anarchist might well shudder
at the thought of employing such an agent
of destruction." It's more a matter
of watching the habitual, how he is the only
one, at the only place, at the only time,
regularly. And access. It takes two weeks
to get that down, and a week for Christmas
to pass, and another week to lay
the trap, and that's a lot of time to spend
in Caldwell, playing a sheep buyer
without enough money to buy a one-eyed
ewe. So all Frank had to do
was open his gate, coming home after work.
He did. It took him an hour to die.

You can go to hell to figure out why I
didn't leave Caldwell, giving Sheriff Nichols
two days to catch me, why I left the makings
in my hotel room, why I didn't hide
my tools and explosives. I swear I've killed
at least twenty before, successful,
clean, no one left to pay any heed to Harry Orchard.
Go figure. Go to hell.

MORE HISTORY: HARRY ORCHARD FINDS A FATHER

IN DETECTIVE JAMES MCPARLAND, PINKERTON

AGENT AND CONFESSOR, JANUARY 23, 1906

"My son, the reason the guard watches
you more than that already condemned
prisoner is that you are such a great
criminal the guard is hypnotized. He simply
has to watch you.

"My son, you are a man of intelligence
and reasoning power, as your forehead
indicates. You possess the ability of doing
a large amount of good, as well
as evil. In first starting out
in the world, had you formed associations
with church-going citizens instead
of socialists, murderers, and anarchists,
you would have been a shining light
in the community. Use your God-graced
intelligence now to follow the right path.

"My son, you need not confess to the murder
of Frank Steunenberg. It would not
surprise me if the Western Federation of Mines
were in on it. The State of Idaho has enough
to convict you. Think of your everlasting

soul. The State can take care of you.
It will have no satisfaction in sending you
to the gallows, you who are nothing more
than the tool of the power behind the throne,
the Inner Circle. Come up and name them
and make a full confession and the State
will tend you."

"My God, if I could place
confidence in you. I want to talk.
Your talk is right. I know every
word you say is true. I am satisfied
that all you have said is for
my own good. I look upon
you as my father for the present."

"My son, if you act in good faith, the State
of Idaho will have its savior in you."

"My father, I killed seventeen
men before Steunenberg. I rigged
a score of explosions. I lit the fuse
to the Bunker Hill explosion
of 1899. All of my crimes
were commissioned by
William Haywood, George
Pettibone, and Charles Moyer
of the Western Federation of Mines.
George Pettibone was my mentor,
instructing me in the ways of hell

fire, how to mix stick phosphorous,
bisulfphide of carbon, benzine,
alcohol, and turpentine."

"My son, the State will cradle you
in its arms of mercy and righteousness."

MORE HISTORY: HARRY ORCHARD FINDS GOD AT THE ADA COUNTY JAIL, JANUARY 24, 1906

Still, he thinks heaven is all
kinesis, and the only way to arrive
is to stop everything, the blue
longing, the elements of desire,
the smooth fit of hate. Killing
a former governor or killing
twenty men is nothing: only
so much lead ignited by a fish-line
trigger, only a poundful of nails.
An explosion stops plenty, but not
enough to get Harry Orchard
to heaven. Beneath heaven, sleeping
men lie above the pulses of silver,
among Pinkerton agents, horses, axes,
and fire, the divisions of love they die
into. Sometimes they wake not
knowing how they came to lie there
in a jail bed, until a woman, the governor's
wife, enters, opening her winged hands
and answering the little human
cry: "God has made heaven, assembling
its architecture larger than all
of us, a room too large to explode."

Harry Orchard stirs. "He's got that
on me," he thinks, shouldering
into sleep. He dreams of the crippled
Christ, a leg broken from bad luck,
the timber support rotted, a cave-in,
and he carries Christ in his arms,
to the blueing light, the powdery
silvered air. And Harry Orchard stops.
At the trial, Clarence Darrow would say
Orchard was too dumb and fearing
to know when to stop confessing. Which
was true. Still, alone in his sleep, Orchard
feels the chill of the winter air converted,
its shock in his chest. The seizing
intimates the cold silence of his sleeping, and
he wakes. He kisses the chain of the crucifix
the widow gave him, twirling the metal
rivulets together, as if
he were braiding blasting wire.

MORE HISTORY: PETTIBONE V. NICHOLS, 203 U.S. 192 (1906)

None of the parties in the Supreme Court case disputed these facts:

"The agent of the State of Idaho [Prosecutor James Hawley and Detective John McParland] arrived in Denver, February 15, 1906, but it was agreed between them and the officers of Colorado that the arrest should be made some time in the night of Saturday, after business hours; that the arrest should be secret and that the accused [George Pettibone] should be clandestinely hurried out of the State of Colorado, without knowledge of his friends or counsel; that he was at his usual place of business during Thursday, Friday, and Saturday, but no attempt was made to arrest him until 11:30 p.m. Saturday, after all courts were closed. Moyer and Haywood were arrested under the same circumstances, without any right to hearing before deportation. Further, between the hours of 5 and 6 o'clock on Sunday morning, February 18, the officers of the State and the militia from the State of Colorado provided a special train and forcibly placed him on said train and removed with all possible speed to Idaho; that prior to removal he requested to be allowed to communicate with his friends and his counsel and his family, and the privilege was absolutely denied him until his arrival in the County of Canyon, State of Idaho, whereupon the 23rd of February, 1906, Pettibone sued out a writ of habeas corpus from the Supreme Court of Idaho."

53

In upholding the circuit court's dismissal of Pettibone's suit, Justice John M. Harlan of Kentucky agreed that while the means of extraditing Pettibone (and Moyer and Haywood) may have violated his constitutional rights, the State of Idaho, in whose possession was the accused, had authority over the accused: "Pettibone is held by Idaho in actual custody under an indictment charging him with a crime against its laws." Regardless how they got there, Pettibone, Moyer, and Haywood were in the hands of the law.

Justice Joseph McKenna of California dissented: "This case is different than the cases cited to support the prevailing opinion. In the case at bar, the States, through their officers, are the offenders. They, by an illegal exertion of power, deprived the accused of a

constitutional right. I submit the facts in this case are different in kind and transcend in consequences those in the case of *Mahon v. Justice*, just as the power of a state transcends the power of an individual. No individual could accomplish what the power of two states accomplished; no individual could command the means and successes; could make arrests of three citizens in their homes; could command the resources of jails, armed guards, and special trains; could successfully time all acts to prevent inquiry and judicial interference. It does not need emphasizing. But how is it when the law becomes the kidnapper. Kidnapping is a crime, pure and simple."

MORE HISTORY: CLARENCE DARROW GIVES HIS CLOSING ARGUMENT, IDAHO V. HAYWOOD, JULY 25, 1907

Somewhere in his eleven-hour speech, Clarence Darrow said:

"I speak for the poor, the weak, for the weary, for that long line of men, who, in darkness and despair, have borne the labors of the human race. The eyes of the world are upon you--upon you twelve men of Idaho tonight. Wherever the English language is spoken and wherever any tongue makes known the thoughts of men in any portion of the civilized world, men are talking and wondering and dreaming about the verdict of these twelve men that I see before me now. If you kill him, your act will be applauded by many. If you should decree Bill Haywood's death, in the railroad offices of our great cities men will applaud your names. If you decree his death, amongst the spiders of Wall Street will go up paeans of praise for these twelve men good and true. In every bank in the world, where men hate Haywood because he fights for the poor and against that accursed system upon which the favored live and grow rich and fat—from all those you will receive blessings and unstinted praise.

But if your verdict should be 'Not Guilty' in this case, there are still those who will reverently bow their heads and thank these twelve for the life and reputation you have saved. Out on your broad prairies where men toil with their hands, out on the wide ocean where men are tossed and buffeted on the waves, through our mills and factories, and down deep under the earth, thousands of men, and of women and children—men who labor, men who suffer, women and children weary with care and toil—these men and these women and these children will kneel tonight and ask God to guide your hearts—these men and these women and these little children, the poor, the weak, and the suffering of the world, are stretching out their helpless hands to this jury in mute appeal for Bill Haywood's life."

After the acquittal, William E. Borah, the prosecutor, said: "All Darrow had to say was no soul corroborated Orchard's confession. We already lost the case."

MORE HISTORY: HARRY ORCHARD SERVES LIFE AND DIES AT THE IDAHO STATE PENITENTIARY, APRIL 19, 1954

I can say only so much as to why,
but you can figure easy how Frank
  Steunenberg deserved it, calling in
      the federal troops on May 2, 1899,

holding the Coeur d'Alenes under
martial law for two years, holding
  nine hundred miners in a bull pen for a month.
      We miners won't forget it, even if we

did commandeer a train, call it
the Dynamite Express, load it up
  with twelve hundred men in Kellogg and Wallace,
      scattering the sixty or so scabs

at the Bunker Hill mine, and blow up
the Sullivan concentrator with three thousand
  pounds of dynamite, and even if
      John Hawker, who helped me set

the fuse line, prophesied rightly,
"You can't steal railroad trains,
  dynamite mines, and burn villages
      without some reaction." What I

didn't count on was that I had to sell
my sixteenth share of the Hercules
   mine when I had to run for British
      Columbia. With a turn of a shovel,

God smiled upon the Hercules, making
May Arkwright Hutton rich and
   respectable from my share. Don't you
      know her plaque faces Bing Crosby's

plaque in the Washington State Hall
of Fame? I still say Big Bill Haywood was
   in on it from the beginning. What
      money I got for my share of

the Hercules, maybe two hundred
dollars, women, gambling, and
   whiskey got it all in a month. Let that be
      a lesson for you. And another lesson:

be a man and take your
punishment. Don't hitch onto
   lawyers to set you free. Forgive
      your captors. Refuse parole, even

when it is handed to you upon
a silver platter. Instead, take up something
   humble, manful, something
      like the sin that got you in the Idaho

State Pen in the first place. Me,
I take a trowel, and scrape clean
   a little dry earth, make holes deep
         enough only for rose bushes, where

   nothing good is in the ground
except for some new life seeking
   the good daylight. Then come spring
         and the flames of red petals that praise

   God's passion in this desert. The only
favor I asked was to be given
   an eastern window, to watch the Jaycees
         build a phosphorescent cross upon Table Rock.

   I am told it will light up the whole
of Treasure Valley with its silver
   glory. The warden, and this is true,
         with tears in his eyes, clasped my hand

   and led me to my new cell, and I kissed
his hand. He is the best man I have
   known. And while I dare not tarry
         into the future, I believe my roses will

   cling forever against this hard rock,
pressing like testament against
   the past, and I thank God, for all
         the good the past has done me.

MORE RECENT HISTORY: IRWIN P. UNDERWEISER,

CHAIRMAN OF BOARD, SUNSHINE

MINING COMPANY, AT THE ANNUAL

STOCKHOLDERS' MEETING, MAY 2, 1972,

IN COEUR D'ALENE

To the stockholders, 9:17 a.m., two hours before the fire:

"While our management is successfully dedicated to growth through internal expansion, mergers, and acquisitions, and while the Sunshine Mine itself made a profit, the corporation must report a net loss of 1.2 million dollars for 1971. These losses, beyond all our control, are due to a write-off in securities and lower silver prices. However discouraging that news is, I am happy to report that the first quarter earnings for 1972 are a healthy $122,000, as the Sunshine Mine has delivered two million ounces of silver. All indications are that we are definitely on the upswing."

Arrives Rogers C. B. Morton, Secretary
of the Interior, and conveys
President Richard M. Nixon's
sympathies. He is tall, white, white-
haired. He offers his own personal
condolences, says that none of this makes
sense, and seeks the widows and
children, and he says, "Yes sir,
this has been considered a safe mine."
President Nixon, that same day,
initials the telegram to the Mayor
of Kellogg, Idaho (unnamed): MAY
GOD BE MERCIFUL ON US. YOU CAN
EXPECT THE FULL SPECTRUM OF
FEDERAL ASSISTANCE. Upon
his return, the Secretary of the Interior
recommends not to declare any
of the counties a major disaster area.
The President brushes the back
of his hand, says, "Right. I will accept that."
Nine days later, Casey Pena and Dan
Taylor are the last exhumed, and the
coroner recorded that Casey died

from the start and that Dan survived
one day longer underground
than Tom Wilkinson and Ron Flory,
but his luck ran out, the fire
not burning itself out until summer.

LAST BIT OF HISTORY: IRWIN P. UNDERWEISER,

CHAIRMAN OF BOARD, SUNSHINE MINING

COMPANY, SPEAKS TO AN ASSOCIATE PRESS

BUSINESS EDITOR, MAY 9, 1972

"In spite of the shutdown, we may make a profit on the closure. Insurance will cover cost of a shutdown of up to six months, although we don't anticipate such a lengthy closure. Also keep in mind that the Sunshine Mine is our nation's largest single silver producer. I wouldn't be surprised if the closure might put a crimp on the silver supply, forcing prices to go up in the ten percent neighborhood."

III. *UNDER GOD*

Maurya: They're altogether this time, and the end is
come. May the Almighty God have mercy on Bartley's
soul, and on Michael's soul, and on the souls of Sheamus
and Patch, and Stephen and Shawn; and may He have
mercy on my soul, Nora, and on the soul of every one who
is left living in the world.

    Michael has a clean burial in the far north, by the grace
of the Almighty God. Bartley will have a fine coffin out
of the white boards, and a deep grave surely. What more
can we want than that? No man at all can be living for
ever and we must be satisfied.

—J. M. Synge, Riders to the Sea

Alice Hillman, like the other
   forsaken, can only dwell
on detail—how her Howard
   died of monoxide asphyxiation

in twenty, maybe thirty
   seconds (the coroner could
be that precise for her)—a way
   to imagine the ninety-one

men, heaped in smoke, dying
   in a cloud. Whenever she
dreams their deaths, it is
   the clawing of rock face

for air, the raw metal taste
   of the self-rescuers in
their mouths, she wakes—No,
   I wasn't there, and she falls

asleep again, dreaming,
   taking her husband's
self-rescuer in her hands,
   throwing it upon a mountain

of self-rescuers. One miner,
   old Avery Killock, tells her,
"You know, Alice, you're lucky
   you don't have to see the bodies."

And then she must describe
    Howard's disfigurements
to distinguish his body among
    the dross: "A scar on his neck

from an accident at
    the Sunshine, and his foot
was crushed in a cave-in
    at Butte. It's all mangled.

And you know, I wonder
    did he die that way? Did
he cry? Was he scared?
    Did he try to climb the walls?

Did he try to dig out?" And
    there's nothing but talk among
them, the histories of accident:
    "And Louis Groos, don't you

remember, he'd been in a car wreck
    and the next day, the second,
he went back to work. He said
    he had a lucky—something—

on his shoulder. Was it
    an angel?"

DEATH BENEFITS

The Sunshine Mining Company cannot be sued, for Idaho law provides that employers may be held liable for only workman's compensation claims. State workman's compensation carries a $750 burial award and a maximum $26,550 for a widow without dependent children, a maximum of $35,400 with three or more children. The company offers a $5,000 life insurance package. And with a union- and company-sponsored compensation fund of $225,000 for the seventy-seven widows, 181 dependent children, and hundreds of laid-off miners, the average widowed family can expect death benefits almost equal to two years of a good miner's salary.

67

This is the First Day of the Rest of Your Life.

Live it Safely.

—Entrance sign for the Sunshine Mine

Safety incentive plan:

for 640 consecutive man-hours without a lost-time accident:

an electric can opener;

for 1280 consecutive man-hours without a lost-time accident:

an electric fry pan;

for 1920 consecutive man-hours without a lost-time accident:

a sleeping bag;

for 2560 consecutive man-hours without a lost-time accident:

a color television.

"It ain't Bob Lowery's fault. He's got

a good heart, even though he's too much

company for my blood. But a safety

engineer at Sunshine has got about

as much say as a mucker. Before

Charley Angel left ten years ago,

our safety never slowed. You'd get

tramped quicker for an unsafe mine

practice than for missing a round

or showing up drunk and laying off.

Since he left, it's get that muck

out or else. Of course, a boss likes

to get muck. That's how
he gets his reputation. Mucking first."

Of course, that was Ira Voigt for you,
and he'd be the best at hoarding the safety
time, lugging home an RCA
for his wife, Kate, and proud to be
the first miner to win the color TV. Two
years and not a scratch, and the young miners,
thinking the prizes are just so much
bullshit, would say, "Yeah, Ira was a slow
mucker. He's stoked out even if he hasn't
broken any bones," dismissing his twenty years
in the mines as so much history. Kate now
turns on the RCA. Walter Cronkite reports
the violence at the Miami convention is nothing
like Chicago in 1968. Richard Nixon is
lifting up Spiro Agnew's arm. Their faces
are clean, almost white and joyful. Kate
thinks if men were angels, their faces would be
that color, the tiniest eyelets of light
through the screen's black mesh. It was Bob
Lowery himself who told Ira the men
were too slow to learn how to use
the self-rescuers, that the turnover
was too quick, "You'd have to retrain the men
every six months, or they would forget
how to use them." And Bob is as good
a man as they get; once he was a theology
student, which comforts Kate a little. At

the convention, the delegates rise, a body
of angels, and above them fall the balloons,
unnetted, and governors and senators
touch them, laughing, singing easy in good
time. For Kate, it is the wind that is hard,
running through the summering willows
Ira planted, intoning the old sexual fugues
brought on, oh Lord, by unsettled love.

LET US SAY THE VANISHED HAVE LEFT SOMETHING

for me, a Pacific wave that surrenders
   its slow way inland, that collapses
      in its own sluice, then retreats

west to the older coasts, that leaves
   pebbles, mica, and shells
      which I will box and shelve

to fill the open shafts. It is how
   the vanished tell me it is
      about time to go. And I will,

soon enough, but these nights
   until then, I will rest, waiting to hear
      the awful turn of the ocean coming,

like God's palm chafing toward
   Idaho. And I wish that it were
      all the voices of the dead I knew

instead of this wave that comes,
   every one of their voices decipherable,
      returning like blood, pumping my own

blood, so that I become still
   in this waiting. That the vanished might
      come and think me dead, even then

they might not be mistaken.

God so temper me.
When I think ascension,
it is the hurl of the icy body,
perfected, to heaven.
But one mile down, among
the rock and rigor-mortised,
it is hard to remember God's
face in the clouds, no more
than the sleight of wind
effacing the under-skiff,
pulling down, and I would
see nothing but the lactating
teats of cows. But how could
a ten-year-old boy submit
such a confession to the other
kids? And so with me, the clouds
were a U-boat, something
my father had fought, and I
could recall each part
from my father's plastic model
in the bottle, especially the dorsal
hull he let me fit, and he steadying
my hand as I held the forceps,
giving the submarine its outer
form. That night I practiced

my signature, playing upon
the variations of D and T,
and nothing worked. I
remember now that extraction
really has do with something else,
something religious, but that
is gone, too. So much muck. So
much grounding. God, so
temper me. Perhaps extraction
begins with Jonah,
or what father called the sign
of Jonah, speaking out in the whale's
great chambering, underwater, deeper
in it than I, and the voice rang out
of the belly, spilling diaphanous
into water, rising to the surface,
into the air. He could hear it,
my father said, as his PT boat
sounded above the ocean. It's hard
not to think of the German sailors,
those whose submarine stalled
in the depth-charge's shock. What
sounding. What sounding.
And no sign of rescue for six
days. It would be easier, cleaner,
to make my own coffin, to return
down the drift to my station
and slide into the stope, take
a breath. It would be easy, if not
for the faces, none of them

angelic. I have come to think
of Christ, although disillusion
awaits all adoration. Even
so, I am given to beseeching
helpless saviors, the infant
Christ, the crucified Christ. It is
the Ascension I cannot grasp.
There is too much earth. My own child,
with his ten months a wounded vein
in me, may be sleeping above me, and I
still tremble to cover him
although I know he will not wake
by a father's disturbance. I come
to kiss the face of the rock.
It is the face of the Christ.
No.
It is my father's face.
No.
And I will not look again,
for I do not want that old retrieval,
but my family: my wife, my child,
my dread, my own, hearing those calls
home, heeding them in heart, and
oh, how nigh is death, and how nigh
are the ringing censers' sounding
of what might be yesterday,
or tomorrow.

1982, 1991-94